The JAG Method

An entrepreneur's journey to personal and professional success

JOHN A. GALLUCCI JR., MS, ATC, PT, DPT

with Jim Waggoner, Kayla George & Stephanie Checchio

DEDICATION

This book is dedicated to my loving family,
Dawn, Stephanie and Charles. You are my inspiration to succeed,
my strength to break down barriers, and the constant support system that
keeps me going. Thank you for always being the best part of me.

PREFACE

John A. Gallucci Jr.'s meteoric rise in the business world has far less to do with personal success than a heart-felt desire to help people realize their own dreams.

That, in a nutshell, is what makes the 55-year-old Staten Island native tick while building a high-energy career that began with $7 in his checking account and a future blueprint for life scribbled on a movie-theatre napkin at the ripe old age of 18.

One of his target groups has been young adults – yes, they've been labeled "Millennials and Generation Z" by sociologists and journalists alike – those 20-30 year olds navigating the early stages of careers who will require wisdom, patience and sound judgment as real-life decisions bear down on them.

Gallucci knows all about that nurturing process. His Northeast-based company — JAG-ONE Physical Therapy — has over 1,400 employees with an average age of 35.

"Our interview process isn't about what your pedigree happens to be…not about what your grades were…not about where you worked…I take the resume, I congratulate them, I turn it over to take notes on the back and ask the person 'Tell me about yourself.' A large percentage will tell me what school they attended or something along those lines. I'll say 'No, tell me something about YOU, engage with me.' Some can sit there for

30 minutes and tell you about themselves and then they'll be smart and ask me, 'Tell me about YOU.'

"Then you're having a conversation. Shouldn't healthcare in general and any specific healthcare field be about people taking care of people and communicating?"

This is the story of John A. Gallucci Jr. and his unconventional and inspiring road to personal and professional success — and the methods he eagerly passes along to other people looking to get started.

He'll tell us the whole story, in his own words, and manage to work in a past 50th birthday meeting with heavy-metal legend and entrepreneur Gene Simmons, the bass guitarist and co-lead singer of the rock band KISS.

It's a story that combines the road less travelled with an unshakable will to succeed, often against large odds. It's about a man who set his heart and mind on becoming a successful businessman — and then followed a plan that got him there.

Hopefully his voice will resonate with our audience — young and old alike — as the president & CEO of JAG-ONE Physical Therapy continues expanding his comprehensive outpatient physical therapy company that has grown to over 125 locations throughout New Jersey, New York and Pennsylvania.

It's a voice that has already been heard — he added the regional Ernst & Young Entrepreneur of the Year to a long list of previous accomplishments — while continuing to be a prolific author/motivational speaker/mentor as well as husband and father of two children.

JAG-ONE Physical Therapy has been the most visible and successfully marketed business of its kind in the Northeast, marked by steady growth, enthusiasm and community involvement. He has been the Medical Coordinator for Major League Soccer since 2007; was an athletic trainer for the New York Red Bulls from 1999-2006; the director of the Sports Medicine Institute for Barnabas Health from 2000-2005; and has worked as an athletic trainer for the New York Knicks, NYU and Columbia University.

He's the former chairman of the New Jersey Governor's Council on Physical Fitness and Sports.

And that's just a sample size of his resume.

John Gallucci Jr. had neither an easy path to success nor a surefire guarantee against failure, but he certainly wasn't afraid to take on challenges or grasp hold of a tenacious work ethic.

"Not bad for a kid from Staten Island," he summarized during a brief introductory conversation late last summer.

We hope you enjoy "The JAG Method" as much as we did compiling the life stories and lessons within these pages.

And, along the way, we hope his words manage to convey the inspiration behind another American success story, one born in the NYC borough of Staten Island that spread its wings into New Jersey, Pennsylvania, and New York.

It's good to know that The American Dream is still alive and well.

Not bad at all, John A. Gallucci Jr. "JAG".

Not bad at all.

TABLE OF CONTENTS

FOREWORD

By Armond Hill and Michael M. Reuter

Armond Hill

I had the pleasure of working with John Gallucci Jr. at Columbia University. He was our athletic trainer for the men's basketball team. The first thing that I noticed about John was his love and passion for taking care of athletes. His commitment to his job, the detail in his care and the personal touch he gave to each, and every student-athlete was outstanding! I remember one particular moment when one of our players was injured in a vicious play on the court. John spent every waking moment that night with that player and today, 20 plus years later, they still have a relationship.

John's book is all about developing relationships with his patients. His work ethic is unparalleled, and it shows in all the examples in this book. Every chapter is a moment in his life, but he leaves you with a message and an example of how you can apply it to your life. In chapters 10 and 11 he speaks of the millennials. It is extremely powerful because he talks to the youth of today about the signs of the times and the future. It is simple (KISS), yet BRILLIANT!

I would be remiss if I did not mention the love he shares with his wife Dawn and family throughout the book. Their humble beginnings, their trust in each other and their plan. I'll have to tell him he wrote an epic love story too!

Armond Hill, Director of Basketball Administration, Indiana Hoosiers,

NBA Champion

* * *

Michael M. Reuter

E xperiential leadership learning at its greatest! The magical keys of extraordinary leadership excellence are captured with passion, intensity and inspiration. With simplicity and poignancy, John's life journey provides an experiential reality of learning and growth, and the extraordinary success that results from them. As in the lives and stories of other great leaders, his life's journey underlines a passionate commitment to discover and realize the gifts of selfless *being*, his *'why'*. It is this great *being* that became the fire of extraordinary *doing*, his *'how'*. It is this passionate commitment to his life's purpose and meaning, one filled with positivity and a relentless pursuit to move himself from life's *'as is'* to an extraordinary *'what can be'* for himself and others.

To life, people and everyone he serves, *"John never says no."* For every reader, there is a special magical treasure. His is the story of a great leader who truly *lives* every day of his life. This is one of his great gifts of inspiration. His story epitomizes the paths taken by highly successful leaders… lives of continuous learning, passionate and relentless pursuit of dreams, boldness and daring in living life's possibilities and serving others to achieve their great potential. This is the stuff of great leadership!

Michael M. Reuter, Director Emeritus, the Buccino Leadership
Institute, Seton Hall University

CHAPTER ONE

FIND YOUR WHY

"When I was about 20 or 21 my family lost everything to bankruptcy and our world collapsed. I had to figure life out — quickly."

John A. Gallucci Jr. knew what he needed to earn his Bachelor's degree ASAP and it didn't matter the major. He admittedly spent more time concentrating on wrestling than academics while in high school.

"I delivered Domino's pizza, was a bouncer at a bar, staying until 2, 3 or 4 in the morning cleaning the bar and toilets to make extra money. That's what I did basically for four years to put myself through school. I'd start at 5:30-6 a.m. studying, then going to my classes before heading to my pizza delivery job.

And, beginning his journey to become an athletic trainer and physical therapist, Gallucci figured he would need an un-reproachable work ethic.

"After earning my undergraduate degree (in Political Science, no less), I knew I had to go to grad school to get the science degrees to become a physical therapist/athletic trainer. So I ended up getting myself a sheet-rocking and painting job and then opened up my own local land-scaping business, which ended up consisting of 40 lawns that I took care of for neighbors at their homes or personal businesses. I became the handyman of my community. I did everything for a couple of years to get through college."

As you can see, I found my "WHY" at a very young age, and every decision I made was strategic in order to attain the goals I set forth for myself. Take the time to truly figure out what you are passionate about, and how you can conform your life to fulfilling that passion each and every day. Hard work, dedication, and perseverance are all qualities that are needed in order to attain your goals. But first, you need to set your goals. Dig deep inside of you, figure out who you want to be and what you want to be remembered for. The path from dreams to success does exist, but first you must find your "WHY".

CHAPTER TWO

WRITE IT DOWN...

G allucci's high school graduation seemed to awaken his drive as he began seriously contemplating his future.

That led to a movie date with childhood sweetheart Dawn and a spontaneous call for action.

"I was 18 and we went to watch Rambo because we got half-price tickets on a restaurant promotion. That night we got there about an hour too early. In that hour, I explained to her our future life (scribbled furiously on a napkin): We would get married; we would both have successful careers; we'd have two children, named Stephanie and Charles; we'd buy a house in New Jersey; we'd open up a physical therapy company that would be named after me and have multiple sites, including an office in Manhattan, because if you can make it there, you can make it anywhere.

"Did I mention that I hadn't even started college yet? Well, on our 25th wedding anniversary, I threw Dawn a big party and gave a speech dedicated to her that outlined how every promise was fulfilled and everything I said had come true."

"Why did it come true? It goes back to the people who inspired me. I surrounded myself with inspirational people who preached the importance of having a strong work ethic."

Fast-forward to 2023, and the Gallucci's have checked off all the boxes.

"I hit 50, and I own a brand, a company, and a culture with over 125 locations and still growing. And I picked one of the most competitive industries in America."

What started as a conversation transformed into the driving force behind my success. I had a plan and I was determined to achieve my goal, despite the various roadblocks along the path. Although it was *my* dream, from the very beginning I knew I was not in it alone. In order to be successful, you must surround yourself with positivity, with people who want to see you succeed and will support you throughout every step of the way. First, write it down, then, build a strong foundation. There will always be people cheering at the finish line, but who is along for the journey?

CHAPTER THREE

FAIL TO SUCCEED

G allucci figured that his best route for success would be to gain hands-on experience prior to and during his post-graduate studies.

"I knew I had to go to grad school to get the science degrees I needed to become a physical therapist and athletic trainer."

But some rejection awaited him.

"We were married four months after I graduated college, because Dawn refused to marry me unless I had a college degree. So, we had a beautiful wedding on Staten Island, but as I applied to a lot of graduate schools (knowing I didn't have straight A's or an undergrad degree in science) I was rejected by a lot of schools."

In order to make lemonade out of those rejection-lemons, he decided to apply for entrance into athletic training programs, where he was conditionally accepted into LIU-Brooklyn, earning the first of two Master's degrees, in athletic training sports science (1993).

"I told Dawn on our honeymoon the good news, that I was accepted into athletic training school, but we knew I wouldn't be able to work a full-time job. We agreed that she would work full-time, and I would work odd jobs pursuing a Master's degree. I was a substitute teacher at numerous schools and continued working as a painter and sheet-rocker."

Gallucci, in fact, had sold his first business — landscaping — to buy his fiancé an engagement ring and later pay for the wedding.

"She had the job with benefits and we were doing all these things just to pay my tuition bills."

Still in their early 20s, climbing the mountain seemed to be a daunting task.

You may have heard the phrase, "you must fail to succeed" and think to yourself, well, what does that really mean? For me, the continuous rejection into physical therapy school is what really made me persevere and keep pushing. If they weren't going to accept me based on my undergraduate academics, what alternative did I have in order to ultimately get myself into school?

They always say, you can't keep doing the same thing over and over again and expect different results. Use failure as motivation and if plan A is not working out, choose an alternate route.

CHAPTER FOUR

USE ADVERSITY TO YOUR ADVANTAGE

G allucci never tires of telling employees the story of how he and his wife struggled to make ends meet as a young married couple.

Once a week they'd stroll down New Dorp Lane, not far from their Staten Island apartment, to shop at a nearby grocery store.

"The store manager knew who we were. We'd come in with these huge envelopes of coupons, a tight budget and a plan on how to survive until the next paycheck. Well, one week we found out I had made a minor accounting error in our checking account and we had $7 left. So, we decided to make a game of it, to go to the A&P supermarket and see if we could live off the $7 for the week. It was a different time in 1991, and I was a very proud guy who wanted to do it on my own, so we took the $7 and our coupons and walked around.

"We found two pounds of pasta for 39 cents, three cans of sauce for 29 cents apiece and some peas ... and the only meat we could afford at the time was cans of tuna fish, like 75 cents apiece. We had this strategic plan and it came out to under $7.

"Dawn realized we didn't have any vegetables and said we had to figure something out. She went to the produce aisle, looked down and there were two $20 bills at her feet.

"She was stunned and brought them to me saying, 'My father and your grandfather have blessed us. They've given us $20 each. We can eat fine this week.' Now, me being the fine Catholic man from Monsignor Farrell HS, I took the money to the manager. But he said he was going to take $40 out of his own pocket and put it in the register. 'If anyone claims it, I'll give it to them. In the meantime, you two kids go buy yourselves a steak or two.' So we took the $40 and put $20 in savings and put the other $20 to good use until the next paycheck."

The unexpected blessing provided a lesson which took root in the young married couple.

"We made a promise to each other that we'd never be in that situation again and that we needed to work harder than anybody else in our careers to succeed. From that day on, we both focused on that — myself as an athletic trainer and Dawn as a paralegal at a law firm — and we wouldn't hesitate to put in 80 hours a week if necessary.

"We were two kids working and hustling as much as we could. We hustled so much that we'd put one full salary away. We knew nothing but work in those early years of wedded bliss."

Everyone falls on hard times, but what life lessons do you learn from your adversity? Are you able to take a step back and use trying experiences as motivation to continue striving for your goals?

Although you may not realize it in the moment, overcoming adversity is actually one of your biggest advantages. When you are faced with adversity you have two options: you can be discouraged or you can have the courage to persevere and get through it. What decision are you going to make?

CHAPTER FIVE

MENTORS MATTER

Gallucci's father ran a medical-supply store in Brooklyn delivering equipment to a medical building that housed the International Longshoremen's Association clientele.

His youngest son, John Jr., would sit for hours watching patients receive physical therapy.

"Physical therapy has been in my heart since I was 13 years old. I would watch with astonishment as the therapists lifted patients from a wheelchair into a tub, work with those people and help them to walk again."

Eventually, his youthful curiosity caught the attention of a particular physical therapist, Sam Feather, who invited John to do odd jobs on a part-time basis after school and on weekends.

"He told me 'You really have a desire to do this. This really interests you.'"

Three years later, at 16 and approaching his junior year in high school, an uncle approached John at a large family get together and struck up a conversation.

"The crux of the conversation was 'What are you thinking about college? What do you think you want to do when you grow up?'"

It turns out that his relative, Rich Giordano, was president and CEO of Sleepy Hollow Physical Therapy in Westchester, N.Y., who also worked as a physical therapist with the New York Rangers. He took an interest in the teenager who had already shown signs of leaning toward the same field.

"He said that when I got my driver's license I should come and stay with him for a summer. That's what I did before my junior year. I lived with Rich Giordano and worked about 75 hours a week. Everything that Rich did, John Gallucci Jr. did. If he went for a three-mile jog at 5 in the morning, I went for a three-mile jog. If he ate Chinese food, I ate Chinese food. If he was too busy to get lunch, I didn't get lunch. Whatever he told me to do I did, in order to learn about physical therapy.

"He gave me books to read about anatomy, biomechanics, exercise… He would observe me while allowing me to engage with the patients. I worked with Rich again the summer before my senior year and then during freshman year in college. For three years in a row I lived in his house, with his family, and commuted to work with him."

"Ultimately, he really opened my eyes to the physical therapy profession."

No matter what path you take in life, there is always someone or something that leaves a lasting impression. In today's day and age, many young adults go off to college with big dreams and aspirations. We all hear about leadership and mentorship programs, but do we take full advantage of our resources?

Mentors provide information and knowledge and can often see where we need to improve, where we often cannot. Mentors serve as your sounding boards, advisors, connectors, and encouragers. Behind every successful person is a mentor that helped shape them throughout their journey. Bottom line, mentors MATTER!

CHAPTER SIX

NEVER SAY NO

In the early years of his career, Gallucci sought advice from many of New York's top athletic trainers and physical therapists, including Mike Saunders of the New York Knicks, Ronnie Barnes of the New York Giants, Arthur Nelson of NYU, Rich Giordano of Sleepy Hollow Physical Therapy, Catherine McWilliams of Fairfax Physical Therapy and Jim Gossett of Columbia University.

He spent four years (1992-95) as an athletic trainer at NYU, followed by another five years (1995-99) at Columbia University. During the same years, he worked as a part-time, summer assistant to Saunders, with the Knicks from 1993-2000.

"Throughout my career I've made it a priority to surround myself with people who have contributed to putting physical therapy and athletic training on the map. I've always sought those opportunities and as a result, my mentors have been some of the best clinicians in the country.

"As an athletic trainer and a businessman, I've been successful in finding mentorship from people coming from very successful backgrounds."

The unpredictability of professional sports coupled with the long hours and road trips involved with athletic training, were beginning to wear on the young family.

"We were planning on a second child so I applied and was accepted into a physical therapy program at Dominican University. Barnabas Health, my employer at the time, had a tuition program and my entire doctorate was paid for by my employer. We already owed about $90,000 in student loans and people would look at me like I was insane. Today it's commonplace."

"Ultimately, what happened was that doors opened for me because of my background working for the MetroStars (now Red Bulls), the Knicks, and strength camps with the New York Rangers as a very young adult. I had employment opportunities a lot of my colleagues weren't getting because I was dipping my toes in a lot of different pools."

At JAG-ONE Physical Therapy, it has become a running joke that "John never says no". "I take every meeting, I consider every opportunity, I listen to every opinion, and I vet out every option. You never know what opportunity may lie ahead just by taking a meeting, so I take them all. I listen, I network, and I take something away from every interaction. That is the only way you grow, not just professionally, but personally as well.

The positions I held throughout the early days of my career weren't for the money, it was for the opportunity. The opportunity to surround myself with reputable organizations and mentors who would then connect me to a larger network. Always look at the bigger picture and embrace each encounter and opportunity. Simply stated, never say no."

CHAPTER SEVEN

OPEN YOUR OWN DOORS

G allucci believes in the power of NETWORKING, and he took lessons learned early in life to the professional level, all the while learning about and maximizing his personality strengths.

"I was working at a large healthcare system as an executive overseeing their sports medicine program with the ultimate goal of bringing patients into the system to take advantage of their first-class physicians and services." To accomplish this, he tapped into the community "by networking with people — a school principal, athletic director, athletic trainer, a councilman, a mayor..."

I was at the healthcare system for about a year-and-a-half and the best compliment I ever received came from the former President & CEO. He pulled me into an office — and I'm like employee number 17,500 out of about 19,000 and had about 30 administrators between me and the top guy — and he says 'I'll tell you, you're EVERYWHERE. I go to a meeting and they tell me John Gallucci's here representing the company. I go to another meeting and I hear the same thing.'

"When I decided to leave after five years and start JAG Physical Therapy, I called up the CEO's assistant and requested a one-on-one meeting. He looked me in the eyes and said 'You could have resigned to 30 people before you came to me.' I said yes, I could have, but I would have missed the chance to sit down with you and learn something…and I want you to respect my decision to start my own business based on the lessons I've learned here."

"He gave me an hour to outline my concept and to explain my business. Then he made some suggestions, offered some ideas and then wished me great success."

"If I hadn't taken the first step [requesting the meeting] I would have missed a golden opportunity."

Gallucci's relentless energy and aggressiveness made a direct impact on the company president.

"Now at that time it was taboo in healthcare to take a large advertisement, or a TV commercial, or a billboard – things that are commonplace today. I wanted to be different and adopted a forward facing strategy to best support our local communities, and be visible to them when it mattered most.

"I think what I learned at a young age, and what I do well, is NETWORK the heck out of things! To meet people and find the appropriate mentors every step of the way on my journey."

Boundless energy and an unwillingness to entertain a fear of failure didn't hurt either.

"I really believe that a lot of people don't understand that success comes from how well you advocate for yourself. And that comes down to how willing you are to network. To me success at any level has to do with OPENING YOUR OWN DOORS by advocating for yourself and networking with people who can help you reach your goals. I've met some of the most prominent healthcare professionals in the United States because of my assertiveness and willingness to do that.

"So when you're a kid growing up in New York and you're becoming an athletic trainer, surround yourself with people who

can help you learn. I've always sought those opportunities and as a result, I've learned from the best mentors available to me."

The best advice I can offer is to always make sure you advocate for yourself. If you are going to wait for someone else to present an opportunity, you will be waiting a very long time. You need to be visible, open your own doors, and show people who you are and what you bring to the table. No-one starts at the top, so as the low man on the totem pole, what are you doing to make yourself stand out amongst the crowd? If you are unwilling to speak up, how are you ever going to be recognized for your opinion?

Hard work and the willingness to go the extra mile are qualities that do not go unnoticed. As a former athlete and a coach, the best athletes were the ones that gave 110% every time they stepped into the game. They may not have been the most talented of the group, but their work ethic was unlike any other, and that is the difference between good and great.

CHAPTER EIGHT

JUST JUMP!

G allucci was an athletic trainer for the New York Red Bulls from 1999-2006, serving as head athletic trainer from 2004-2006 and during the latter stages of that stint (he also was the Director of Barnabas Health's Sports Medicine Institute from 2000-2005), he had amassed a clientele from the everyday world.

It was time to spread his wings — with JAG Physical Therapy. The first facility opened in West Orange, N.J., in 2005.

"I signed a lease and we decided to see patients there. I would be with the Red Bulls in the morning, at the West Orange office later, and I would travel with the team on the weekends.

I engaged with the people in the league (Major League Soccer), talking to them about policy issues, which I had a background in through my previous experience as an administrator at Barnabas Health. I needed a full-time physical therapist and hired Mike Evangelist, who came in two weeks before I left with the team for training camp. I tossed him the keys and said, 'Don't put us out of business...patients will keep coming.'

I was on the phone with Mike every day, going over patient care, business strategies and grassroots marketing, and we literally built the business from the ground up. There were 33 facilities around us and I was told I'd be out of business in 10 months."

"We proved those predictions wrong."

As scary as it may seem, there are moments in life when we need to pack up our fears, throw them on our back and JUST JUMP into the unknown. In the initial moments of your free fall you may be frightened and uncertain of your path or target. However, it is in these moments that you must stay calm and remember to open your parachute, consisting of your past experiences, knowledge and network. With the support of your 'parachute' the uncertainty of your free fall will come to an end and you will be better equipped to focus in on your target and eventually land on stable ground.

Take it from someone who has done it before... Go Ahead, JUST JUMP!

CHAPTER NINE

KEEP IT SIMPLE, STUPID

When it came to naming Gallucci's business, the prospective owner consulted a friend in the sports marketing world.

"He sent us 30 names and they were all difficult."

The list was trimmed to 25 and the day came to fill out the legal documents.

"I'm filling out the document to incorporate and at the top it has my full name...John Anthony Gallucci. So, I turnaround to my wife, Dawn and asked 'Why don't we call it JAG Physical Therapy, using my initials?' She said 'You're a genius,' and she's never called me a genius again.

"I didn't want it to be a difficult name to say or remember — John Gallucci Physical Therapy Company...that's difficult. People overthink the simple things when starting a business. There has to be analytics, of course, on the business side, but if you look at physical therapy, what is it? It's people taking care of people. It shouldn't be difficult to talk to people, to motivate people, to rehabilitate people.

"So, we keep it simple ..."

Overthinking is the master of the art of procrastination and creator of problems that were never truly there. It turns the possible into the impossible and the natural into the unnatural. It makes us lose focus on the task at hand and almost never produces optimal results. Therefore, it is imperative that in moments of doubt we choose simplicity. Simplicity, however, should not be confused with easy. Simple is complex. It takes work to strip a problem or decision down to its core and face it head on without any outside influence, but once you get there, your solution will be possible and it will be natural, simply because it was simply yours to begin with...

CHAPTER TEN

LEARN TO LET GO

G allucci has a heart to help guide Millennials to discover and fulfill successful professional lives.

"These are the young adults born between 1980 and 1999: They're not only here but they're the most diverse generation in U.S. history. They have more college degrees and more generational debt than anybody else.

"There are currently 80-100 million in the work force full-time and this generation has technological skills that some of us will never achieve. My 18-year-old son Charles runs a computer better than I do and my 27-year-old daughter Stephanie is at the point where if there's something I can't figure out on my iPhone, she rips it out of my hands."

"Millennials," he said, "are willing to learn".

"What we need to be teaching our youth, young adults and young professionals is that a title doesn't mean success. Their actions are what defines success — you need to be at work on time, to be self-motivated, assertive and self-advocating. Goals of personal, professional and financial growth are what define a person's success.

"Millennials want to lead. They may not understand that it's a process, but they want to lead. And they think outside the box."

"The question I have for business leaders is: how many of you can MOTIVATE and DELEGATE, as opposed to DICTATE? That's a lesson in itself."

Letting go isn't giving up, it isn't forgetting, and it isn't a sign of weakness. Letting go requires bravery, strength and the ability to afford your knowledge to those who surround you. No matter if you are letting go of the bad or for the good, the act in itself makes room for future growth. Like releasing a balloon, it is only after you let go that you will realize that the more you let go, the higher it will rise, and it's absence will allow you to move ahead.

So...take a deep breath and LET GO!

CHAPTER ELEVEN

SUCCESS BREEDS SUCCESS

G allucci recognizes the pressures of living in today's society.

"I think we live in a very competitive, hostile, aggressive society. The stresses of everyday life here in America, whether it be the political scene, or our safety in society...I think we all have a lot of stress to deal with. But I have an underlying philosophy to see the good in people and see ways we can help each other on a day-to-day basis."

And what about those problematic days when everything seems to go wrong?

"Everybody has bad days, but it's how you react to the bad day. If you start off on a bad note and you keep it sour, it's going to stay bad. But if you do things to make it better, the day is going to end better. I think adversity is life's way of challenging you to work harder and be better."

Success breeds further success. At first glance this makes logical sense, but how is it accomplished? The answer may be confidence. At first when we are trying something new, like learning to ride a bike, we may be timid and appear unconfident so we employ our training wheels. However, with practice and support by others our confidence builds, success slowly appears on the horizon and we are no longer in need of those training wheels. Without training wheels and with our newfound confidence, it is now time to apply this skill you have mastered and to pass along your knowledge to help another find the same success.

CHAPTER TWELVE

REMAIN A STUDENT

G allucci uses the lessons he learned from being a team member and believes that the team dynamic works in most endeavors for the benefit of all involved. Every defeat can be turned into victory.

"I came out of a high-level testosterone, confident, aggressive environment of being a wrestler at an all-male high school. It was a competitive winner-takes-all mindset, and it wasn't until later that I began to understand that you can't win every match and every game. When you lose, that can provide the best lessons to making you a better winner.

"I think if you win all the time, you get very lonely, and if you're doing it by yourself, it's not as much fun as when you're doing it with a lot of people.

Time has taught him some valuable lessons.

"I think I'm still a pretty assertive, reactive guy, but I learned some of those lessons and tried to tone down my aggressiveness. I'm able to take a step back and see the whole picture in order to make an educated decision."

The phrase I am choosing to leave you with as we conclude this chapter is 'Be a Sponge'. As a sponge, each day you will choose to 'soak up' or absorb as much knowledge as possible. You should then 'wring out' or afford this knowledge to those who surround you. This cycle should continue always, as there is always someone who can teach you something and another who is waiting to be taught by you. Life is filled with teachable moments; we must learn to embrace them.

CHAPTER THIRTEEN

TAKE TIME FOR YOURSELF

How's this for a 50th birthday present?

Gallucci's closest friends and family, helped arrange a face-to-face meeting with Gene Simmons of the Rock and Roll Hall of Fame heavy-metal band KISS.

"When I was a young kid I really liked KISS. I followed his (Simmons) career and was fascinated by his marketing prowess. I was inspired by Gene Simmons' concept of Keeping It Simple Stupid! It's about relating to people and finding out what they want to engage with. Marketing today is designed to get a product in front of people simply…to be able to advertise it and sell it.

"When we look at my business and my brand, we marketed JAG Physical Therapy (now JAG-ONE Physical Therapy) for people who are active because aren't we all trying to be active? The thought behind my brand is we've sold a component to give you back your activities of daily living, thus our tag-line: "Get Back The Life You Love!"

Gallucci's time with Simmons was put to good use.

"I've been a KISS fan since I was 11 years old. I love rock and roll and I thought they were a little crazy, a little different from everybody else. I've always wanted to learn more about how he built the band and the brand. I picked his brain for an hour-and-a-half and we talked about his business philosophy and how he named the band.

Almost everything will work again if you unplug it for a few minutes; including you! Think about it in terms of your electronics. When our televisions or computers are not working we unplug them and when our cell phones have a frozen screen we turn them off for a few minutes before turning them back on. This usually does the trick, right? So, why aren't we applying these same principles to ourselves? Similar to your electronics, a long time is not necessary, and a few minutes in your office with the lights off and the door closed or a short yoga session can make a world of difference. When we fail to take time for ourselves, it's not a matter of IF we will burnout; it's a matter of WHEN.

CHAPTER FOURTEEN

STAY TRUE TO YOU

G allucci said he welcomes the responsibility entrusted to him of running an expanding business.

"I believe I'm responsible not just for the success of developing and enriching my children, but for the drive and success of the employees I've brought into the company. I have built a culture where every employee has an opportunity for growth - personally, professionally and financially."

On a deeper level, he sees a need to embrace life.

"I think that we've been given a gift of life and as human beings we need to appreciate every breath we take; we need to assist our fellow man along their journey. We can choose to care about others and lend a hand, and we can teach and help develop others."

As we come to the end of this book, I wanted to leave you with a phrase that sums up all of the advice I have given you throughout these chapters; STAY TRUE TO YOU. Along your path there will be many people who will try to change your mind, alter your ideas or tell you it's not possible. IGNORE THEM. It is only you who knows your 'WHY' and it will be you in the end who you will silently thank when you have achieved your dreams. As stated by James Leo Herlihy, "Be yourself. No one can ever tell you you're doing it wrong."

JOHN GALLUCCI JR.'S
WORDS TO LIVE BY

*"My grandfather used to say: 'The best way for a man to measure his wealth is how healthy and happy he is.' I've taken that concept from him and believe that success has nothing to do with money and everything to do with happiness and health."

*"There's always going to be happiness in our lives, but we have to be able to find it. Too many people find the negatives and want to hop on them."

*"I think people who succeed can't be negative. If you want to be a success, you have to be positive."

*"I have built a culture where every employee has an opportunity for growth personally, professionally and financially."

*"Shouldn't healthcare in general and any specific healthcare field be about people taking care of people and communicating?"

*"I surrounded myself with inspirational people who preached having a strong work ethic."

*"We were two kids working and hustling as much as we could. We hustled so much that we'd put one full salary away. We knew nothing but work."

*"I had opportunities a lot of my colleagues weren't getting because I was dipping my toes in a lot of different pools."

*"As a physical therapist and a businessman, I've been successful in finding mentorship from people coming from very successful backgrounds."

*"I think the best advice I've ever received came from my wife Dawn. She said 'Did you ever think about taking a step back and really looking at a situation before you attack?"

*"I think adversity is life's way of challenging you to work harder and be a better person."

*"The stresses of everyday life here in America, whether it be the political scene, or our safety in society … I think we all have a lot of stresses to deal with. But I really have an underlying philosophy to see the good in man and see ways we can help each other on a day-to-day basis."

———————